My Rambles in Upper Wharfedale

A unique reproduction of a fascinating Edwardian lantern lecture illustrated by prints of over 100 of its large glass slides, edited by the author's grandson, Dr Michael L Ryder, and with recent photographs by Barrie Pepper.

Front cover photograph: Kilnsey; *Back cover photograph:* the author at Buckden

My Rambles
in Upper Wharfedale
"Queen of the
Yorkshire Dales"

by

Thomas Ryder
(1867-1950)

Shortened Text of
Edwardian "Limelight Lecture"
(version dated 1907)

Typed on a word-processor by his grandson
Dr Michael L Ryder during 1997

With additional recent photographs by Barrie Pepper
and a foreword by Dr W R Mitchell, MBE

White Rose II, Southampton

First published in 2002
by White Rose II (the imprint of Michael L Ryder) Southampton

A CIP record for this publication
is available from the British Library

ISBN 0950610623

Distributed by:
Kingfisher Productions, The Dalesmade Centre,
Watershed Mill, Settle, North Yorkshire BD24 9LR

Other White II Rose Publications:
Sheep and Wool for Handicraft Workers (1978)
Cashmere, Mohair and Other Luxury Animal Fibres for the Breeder and Spinner (1987)

Barrie Pepper publication:
with Jack Thompson, *Walkers, Writers and Watering Holes: A gentle wander down Wharfedale.*
Wharncliffe *(2000)*

Contents

Foreword

I have a fellow feeling for Thomas Ryder, whose work appears in this book. I left school early, continuing my education through journalism and in due course being invited by Harry Scott to join him on the magazine he had founded, which was also, in effect, an invitation to become a freeman of the Yorkshire Dales.

My first jaunts into Upper Wharfedale were, like those of Thomas Ryder, in part by public transport and in larger part on foot, which is the best way to see the delectable region and to meet its people.

A "magic" lantern and heavy glass slides became familiar to me. In their wooden box, they were unbearably heavy. The projector I used was of grand Victorian proportions, originally operated by limelight and running so hot that one might almost fry eggs on it. At Hetton, an effusive Methodist minister, advancing needlessly across the chapel schoolroom tripped over the wire connecting the lantern to the electricity supply, with the result that the huge bulb was yanked from its position and bounced several times. Needless to say, that evening I had simply to talk.

I am glad that Michael, Thomas's grandson, in preparing the book, has kept to the spirit of the slide show, retaining the romantic title and not making significant alterations to the original text. Older readers will recall the circumstances of the old-style lantern lecture. Young readers – with their hi-tech apparatus – will marvel at the tenacity and skill that brought such a lecture into being.

I wish the book every success.

W R Mitchell (former Editor of *The Dalesman*)

Introduction

Notes by the author's grandson

My grandfather, Thomas Ryder (1867-1950) a tailor of Leeds, was a keen walker and photographer and his limelight lecture entitled *My Rambles in Upper Wharfedale* is based on his walks and his own photographs taken with a large plate camera and processed by himself. It used most of the 250 three-inch by three-inch glass slides he had prepared. These were carried in a stout wooden box that I can hardly lift when full let alone carry. The text of the 1907 version, from which he would read, has 133 pages written in copper-plate handwriting with prints of the slides pasted opposite the text. The first page is here reproduced in facsimile. On the last ten pages of his book are pasted press-cuttings reporting the talk. The first of these is dated 1888 and the last 1945, when I had heard my grandfather speak after which he gave me the slides and the book with the text. I gave a shorter version of the lecture myself after his death in 1950 and before I left Leeds in 1960. Thanks are due to my father, Cecil, for keeping the slides and adding his own notes while I was abroad.

This unique personal account is an important historical and social document full of fascinating original stories about the people of Upper Wharfedale at the turn of the nineteenth century. The start of the "rambles" at Bolton Abbey was reached by train via Ilkley or Skipton. Transport up the Dale was by horse-drawn wagonette, which my grandfather termed the "Mail Coach" and this left behind a cloud of white dust from the metalled, but not tarred, road. After that one really had to walk in those days, and he carried all the heavy photographic equipment himself. This was too obvious to be mentioned in the talk. The route was similar to the modern Dales Way.

I was born in Leeds in 1927, and although my grandfather took me across Ilkley Moor at the age of 10, I discovered Upper Wharfedale myself through a profound period of war evacuation to Buckden House with Leeds Grammar School during 1941. I later walked and cycled further afield in the Dales. I have travelled the world, living for a while in Australia and for 25 years in Scotland, but think that there is nowhere quite like the Dales, although since 1960 I have not often been able to visit the area. I have been taken back in recent years by my sister and her husband specifically to check on changes for this publication and have added brief notes on these which are shown in italics and square brackets. I can report that all the pub names are unchanged in 100 years! I am grateful to Barrie Pepper for taking some photographs of the same views during 2001 and 2002 to show how little has changed.

In editing the text on a word-processor to shorten the length I have left out the entire references to particular slides so that the English of what is used remains in the original form. Most errors of grammar or spelling have been left. There are surprisingly few errors for someone with no secondary education (and no spell checker!). It must also be remembered that these were his own notes not meant to be read by anyone else. Any dates given are those on the slide, but the photographs were often taken several years earlier. A disproportionate amount of space was originally devoted to Bolton Abbey at the outset, but this is the only place most people in the audience were ever likely to visit (by rail, which we used to do as a family certainly as late as the 1940s before the advent of the private car and the closure of such branch lines). Only a few of the 25 slides of the Littondale branch of the Dale have been included. I am grateful to Dr. W. R. Mitchell, MBE, former editor of *The Dalesman* for writing a foreword.

Michael L Ryder, Southampton, 2002

Footnote (1) – What is a limelight? Limelights were originally used in theatres during the nineteenth century, a brilliant, white light being produced by heating lime until it was incandescent. In the theatre this was done by igniting streams of oxygen and hydrogen directed onto a piece of lime. In my grandfather's "lantern" (projector) the heat would have been provided originally by a coal-gas flame and later by an electric arc. For my use my father and I fixed an electric bulb within the lantern. Unfortunately I sold the lantern when I went to Australia.

Footnote (2) – Some of the prints (but not the slides) show named members of The Armley and Wortley (Leeds) Photographic Society, on excursions up the Dale. My grandfather gave the lecture to the Society in 1944, but it appears to be no longer in existence.

ARMLEY DISTRICT NURSING FUND.

President: Rd. Wilson, Esq., J.P.   *Treasurer:* Marshall Stables, Esq., J.P.

:: A LIMELIGHT ::
Lantern Lecture

Will be given in aid of the above Fund,

On TUESDAY, FEBRUARY 18th, 1913,

In the Parochial Hall, Ridge Road, Armley

(by kind permission of the Vicar and Churchwardens),

ENTITLED :—

'My Rambles in Upper Wharfedale'

— BY —

Mr. THOMAS RYDER

(of the Armley and Wortley Photographic Society).

SYNOPSIS OF LECTURE.

A brief description of the beauties of this most favoured valley.
"The Queen of Yorkshire Dales." Its romantic surroundings, its natural scenery, its historical associations, and its strange legendary tales and traditions.
The long and beautiful track of romantic seclusion, stretching from Bolton Abbey through the mountain wilds of Langstrothdale to the great moorlands of the mighty Cam Fells above Oughtershaw, with occasional divergences to such places of note as may be worthy of attention.

Chair to be taken at 8 p.m., by

C. DARLING, Esq., B.A.

(Head Master of the West Leeds High School).

ADMISSION: 6d.; A few Reserved Seats, 1s.

Tickets may be had from Dr. Thos. H. Waddington, Highthorn, Moorfield Road; also the members of the Armley Photographic Society; the collectors of the Nursing Fund; and the Secretary,
JAMES BAXTER, 32, Eyres Terrace, Stanningley Rd., Armley.

Birdsall & Co., "Armley and Wortley News" Office (Soc.), 164, Tong Road.

Limelight Lecture.

My Rambles in Upper Wharfedale.
"The Queen of Yorkshire Dales."
Thos. Ryder. 1907.

Mr. Chairman, Ladies and Gentlemen,

The great majority of
people who annually visit Bolton Abbey
and Woods, after feasting their eyes upon
the rural beauty and loveliness which their
abound seem to have a notion that they
have seen all the beauties which Upper
wharfedale possesses. It is with a
desire to remove that impression, and to
bring other less known but equally delightful
parts of this most favoured valley under
notice that I have laboured to get this
series of Photographs together; to me, it
has been a labour of love and pleasure,—
let us hope it will be a pleasure to you
to review on the Screen. There is
no more delightful valley excursion in

Limelight Lecture

My Rambles

in Upper Wharfedale

"The Queen

of the Yorkshire Dales"

Thos. Ryder, 1907

*M*r. Chairman Ladies and Gentlemen.

The great majority of people who annually visit Bolton Abbey and woods, after feasting their eyes upon the rural beauty and loveliness, which there abound, seem to have a notion that they have seen ALL the beauties which Upper Wharfedale possesses. It is with a desire to remove that impression, and to bring other less-known, but equally delightful parts of this most favoured valley under notice, that I have laboured to get this Series of Photographs together; to me, it has been a labour of love and pleasure – let us hope that it will be a pleasure to you to review on the screen. There is no more delightful valley excursion in the whole broad county of Yorkshire than Upper-Wharfedale – through which it will be my pleasure to guide you on an imaginary ramble.

John Bartholomew map of the area (reproduced from *Tramps and Drives Around Skipton, Grassington and Malham* by Harry Speight, 1902)

Map of Upper Wharfedale [1]

The river Wharfe rises some two-and-a-half miles above Oughtershaw, under Cam Fell, amidst scenes of stern solitude and moorland grandeur, 1273 feet above the level of the sea.

Down to Buckden it is a mountain stream, tumbling over the rocks in a series of cataracts, very fine when the river is flooded.

Below Kettlewell the limestone escarpments on either hand form a remarkable series of terraces, buttressing the green slopes above and below them.

From its source to its junction with the river Skirfare, near to Kilnsey – a distance of some 12 miles – its fall is upwards of six-hundred feet, herein the reason for the rapid rise of this river in stormy weather.

After passing "lovely Burnsall" the river sweeps on its winding way past the Tower and Woods of Barden and thence flows through rocky woodland, and combines to form scenes, sweet, beautiful and grand – passing the Old Priory and its graveyard, where lie all that is left of the warrior, priest and crusader of past centuries.

The entire course of the river is full of rare charm, a charm which in variety of scenic beauty, historic interest, and old world life, cannot be surpassed by any river-valley in the kingdom.

Starting from Bolton Abbey, we follow the river's course to Appletreewick, where we make our first detour in order to pay a visit to Trollers Gill. Then forward to Hebden where we take a rough scramble up the wild and rocky ravine as far as the old lead mines on the vast moorland above Grassington.

At Kilnsey we leave the Wharfe, and follow the river Skirfare up the beautiful vale of Littondale. At Buckden a short two miles brings us to the hamlet of Cray, behind which is the delightful Cray Gill, with its beautiful waterfalls. Thence forward through Langstrothdale and on to the Cam Fells above Oughtershaw.

Suppose then, we have arrived at Bolton Abbey by train, which is the very best and the most convenient starting point for a tour of the upper dale, we saunter out of the railway station, and make our way direct to the Old Priory. It is a charming scene that opens out as soon as we leave the roadway. Having taken in the glorious prospect we descend at once the grassy slope towards the river and stepping stones, the longest footway, of this nature, in England.

Bolton Abbey from the East [2]

The Old Priory stands proud and beautiful in decay, in a green meadow, where stately trees adorn the gentle undulations, the Wharfe rippling cheerfully past, coming forth from wooded hills above, and continuing between wooded hills below. Bolton Abbey is a household word. It seems familiar to us beforehand, we picture it to our minds, and our imagination must be extravagant indeed if the picture is not realised. *There is no longer a rope "handrail" for the stepping stones.*

South side of East end of choir Bolton Abbey, 1906 [3]

The priory is now but a mere relic of what it was, yet it is still a most interesting one of the religion of our fathers. It is a remnant of the faith which the English people cherished during many centuries, and these old ruins, which fold within their embrace the dead of many generations, speak to us of human hopes, fears, affections, and sympathies long since stilled.

Bolton Hall through the South Transept Arch [4]

It is very interesting to wander round the ruins of the Old Priory, – better known probably than any other ruin of its kind in Yorkshire, and gaze in wonderment upon its broken ivy covered walls. It is said that service has been held here uninterruptedly for seven hundred years. *A notice now gives the period as 850 years. The nave of the abbey became the parish church after the dissolution of the monasteries by Henry VIII.*

Ancient Archway [5]

Now labelled as 10ft 9in high and has no greenery. The ancient archway behind the Old Hall, is the remains of the Priory Aqueduct, destroyed by the Scots after Bannockburn, and which was used to convey water from

the western hills to the wheel of the flour mill of the Priory. *The road was metalled Macadam - untarred broken stones and dusty.*

Cavendish Memorial Fountain [6]

Remains unchanged. A few hundred yards away is the beautiful fountain, erected in 1886 by public subscription of the electors in the West Riding of Yorkshire, to the memory of Lord Frederick Cavendish, whose brutal murder in Phoenix Park on May 6th 1882 sent a thrill of horror through Britain. Mr Gladstone said - "He went out as Chief Secretary to Ireland, full of love to that country, full of hope for her future, full of capacity to render her service."

But you will turn again and again to the abbey to gaze on its tall arches, the great empty window, and the crumbling walls, over which hang rich masses of ivy - and walking slowly round you will discover the points whence the ruins appear most picturesque.

Whether it be historically accurate or not to say that the Priory was founded by the Lady Adeliza [*Alice*] de Romille when mourning for the loss by drowning in the rocky strid, of her son - "The Boy of Egremond", long centuries since, uncritical people are content to accept the story of "endless sorrow", as told in Wordsworth's poem, and see in it, and in the "White Doe of Rylstone", little histories which they would rather not have proved wrong in time or circumstance.

We now leave the beautiful old Priory and its surroundings and make our way across the pastures to the woods and river. Of course it is not everyone amongst the crowds of admiring visitors who look upon the scene with an artists eye or a poets thoughts. For example, it was said quite recently of a couple of working women from a West Riding town, who were observed gazing intently upon the beautiful and expansive surroundings – said one of them after a few minutes pause: – "Aye – Hah dus ta like it Peggy?"

"Aye," responded Peggy, with apparent unconcern, "its all reight, yer knaw, but what a grand spot for hanging aht clooaths."

Winter Scene.

Bolton Woods 1908 [7]

The Strid (Bolton Woods) [8]

Presently we come to a narrow, irregular, rocky channel of between four and five feet wide and about sixty feet in length; This is the Strid, or Striding place. Through this narrow passage the Wharfe, which only a few yards higher up is fifty wide, passes, except in flood times, when the entire bed of the river is covered. The waters rush down into the abyss and are caught up again and then carried forward through the wild ravine so impetuously and fearfully as on that day, seven centuries ago, when the "Boy of Egremond" took his fatal leap –

> *"He sprang with glee, for what cared he*
> *That the river was strong, and the rocks were steep.*
> *But the greyhound in the leash hung back*
> *And checked him in his leap.*
> *The boy is in the arms of the Wharfe,*
> *And strangled by a merciless force;*
> *For never more was young Romille' seen*
> *Till he rose a lifeless corpse."*

It is probable that the leap had been made many times before; it has been made many times since. It was the sudden check by the greyhound in his leash which, according to the legend, caused "The Boy of Egremond" to fall back into the abyss; but a mistep of any kind at such a terrible spot would prove fatal. It is foolhardiness and not courage, which would tempt one to change from one side of the Wharfe to the other at the Strid.

Jumping the Strid 1 [9]

I myself have seen men and boys, and even young ladies jump across in daring fashion. This young man is taking the leap quite easily.

Jumping the Strid 2 [10]

Here's another one – look at his sails spread out.

This young man got himself in a rather perilous position. After jumping across quite easily, just to let his friends see how clever he was, he wanted to return, but he found the return journey was not so easy to accomplish. So he jumped on a large rock, a little lower down in mid stream. Here he was in a terrible fix, he could neither get forward nor

backward, as both were dangerous uphill jumps. After playing the 'goat' awhile to the evident amusement of a large crowd of spectators, it was plainly visible he was becoming very uneasy, and when told to make an effort and give a good jump, he said – the rock was so slippery, and his shoes having become very wet by the splashing of the water he could not get a firm footing, and he was afraid he would "drop i t'hoil" if he ventured. Subsequently a rope was thrown to him by the assistance of which he was prevented from slipping back into the water.

Visitors at the Strid (1906) [11]

The rocks about this mysterious gorge are waterworn, and full of round holes, varying from a few inches to a yard in diameter; but the rocks are not merely water worn, they are footworn. The tread year by year of innumberable visitors has polished the great blocks until they are smooth on their upper surface as stepping stones. Here the visitors sit upon them and gaze in wonderment upon the beautiful surroundings while the waters rush turbulently on beneath them. *Few people walk to this spot today.*

View from Pembroke Seat [12]

From here, above the strid, the view is similar today. Trees and river and green clad hills looking charming before us and bid us welcome to the beauties of the upper dale. Here we have a distant view of Barden Tower. The ruined castle of the Cliffords. "The Stout Lord Clifford that did fight in France". But 'stout' is unfortunately not the only name applied to this historical name. After the battle of Wakefield, when the victory was won, the second son of the Duke of York, (who had fled with his tutor from the conflict) was stopped on the bridge, his name was demanded by his pursuers, and quite unable to speak from his fear, the youth fell upon his knees, held up his hands craving for mercy. His tutor in the hope of saving him, cried out - "The son of the Duke of York." "Then" said the ruffian Lord Clifford - "as thy father slew mine, so will I slay thee, and all thy kin." He then plunged his dagger into the body of the inoffensive youth, and commanded the tutor to go and bear the tidings to the widowed mother. For this and other barbarities this Clifford acquired the name of "The Butcher".

Barden Tower. Front [13]

But the ruined pile before us was the residence of a more illustrious and honoured Clifford, better known as the "Shepherd Lord". His love for the pastoral life he had led, was strong within him, and he choose quite Barden for his home. He remained here almost entirely, giving to all in the neighbourhood the example of a useful, peace-loving, and contented life. A quaint inscription over the south door, tells that "it had layne ruinous ever since about 1589" until 1658, when the Ladye Anne Clifford repaired it. The Ladye Anne has left as sweet a memory as her ancestor the Shepherd Lord. Dr Whittaker [1812] says – "her house was – a school for the young, a retreat for the aged, an asylum for the persecuted, a college for the learned, and a pattern for all."

The tower is unsafe to enter, but the adjacent 15th cent. priest's house now houses a tea room. In the 1950s it had trees growing on the walls.

Taking the road behind the Tower, we again come to the river Wharfe.

Barden Bridge [14]

Here we obtain a grand view of Barden Bridge. It is a picturesque three arched structure with angular buttresses, and an inscription, – "This bridge was repaired at the charge of the whole West Riding – 1676". It is 400 feet above the level of the sea, and the road over it is the Skipton and Pateley Bridge highway.

Howgill Bridge (Hough Woods) [15]

Continuing our course by the field path near to the river side, in about two miles from Barden we come to Howgill bridge, at the entrance to Hough Woods, near Appletreewick. This bridge is one huge tree trunk about 90 feet long. *The log came from Newfoundland and the bridge was washed away in a flood during 1936 and during the 1940s could be seen lying at the side of the river further downstream. It was never replaced. The woods were partially felled during World War II. I made an oak-framed enlargement of this photograph into a firescreen.*

Leaving the river side awhile to take a peep a the the old time village of Skyreholme, Percival Hall and Trollers Gill. Presently we come by the stream which flows from Trollers Gill, and a little to the right of this stream we behold Percival Hall.

Percival Hall [16]

Known locally as 'Parse' or 'Passable' Hall. *At that time a farm.* The date over the doorway is 1671. It is Jacobean [*c.1600*] in style and full of interest from its curious old mullions, and former associations. Tradition says that the hall was once the hiding place of the notorious highwayman

William Nevison. *Now called "Parcevall" Hall and used as a Retreat for the Diocese of Bradford; only the gardens are open to the public.*

Appletreewick. Simon's Seat in distance (1906) [17]

The place is of great antiquity. The High Hall at the top of the village street was once the residence of Sir William, and Lord John Craven. William Craven, born [*in 1548*] of humble parents left his native home at a very early age and journeyed to London, on the cart of a common carrier, the journey occupied three weeks. In course of time by industry, perseverance, and integrity he raised himself to very high positions, and in 1611 William Craven became Lord Mayor of London, and subsequently obtained the honour of knighthood.

Sir William Craven was Lord Mayor of London in 1610 and 1618 and is supposed to have provided the basis for the legend of Dick Whittington. His son became a Baron (Earl of Craven) and built Ashdown House in Oxfordshire, which remained in the family until the 1920s. An oak tree has been planted outside High Hall in memory of John Beecroft Lofthouse who farmed there from 1926 until 1970.

Monks Hall (Appletreewick) [18]

Passing down the village street we come to a curious old building, once used it is said by the monks of Bolton. But that is very doubtful for the structure is only

early Jacobean. *Probably the site of the building acquired by the monks in 1300; later used as pigeon cote; now named "Mock Beggar Hall".*

Appletreewick (looking down the village) [19]

Looking down the village street this little uphill place has a charm and beauty wholly its own. Note the small sign on the end of the last building on the right. This is the New Inn, my headquarters when touring

the district. *Again the rough nature of the un-tarred road is clear. There is a striking difference today with flowers, shrubs and trees in the front gardens.*

Burnsall [20]

After a most enjoyable tramp we obtain our first view of Burnsall "The Gem of Wharfedale". With its ancient Church pleasantly placed on rising ground overlooking the village snugly ensconced in the western banks of the Wharfe. Opposite the Red Lion Hotel is the village green, where one is often tempted to idle away the morning watching the rippling river, or eyeing the village people

as they wander to and fro.

Red Lion Hotel. Burnsall [21]

While lazily lounging about here a tramp, a born tramp, comes loafing towards us along the river's bank – a genuine tramp, with a slouch that is born in a man like any other form of genius. He has a sleep eye, which hides its alertness craftily – a sad but uncomplaining face - trousers pockets that gape a little at the seams through perpetual friction of his hands. To look at him, you would suspect some unforgotten tragedy which had killed his hopes, yet left him brave to live out the drear remainder of his life. He approaches the seat by a zigzag devious way, and holds out a dirty palm, a dirty half-penny lies snugly in the palm, and I stare at him in wonderment.

"Mebbe you could'nt sell me a ha'porth o'baccy?" he says gloomily.

"Sell you a —," I begin.

"Ay", he goes on, not heeding the interruption. "its all t'brass I've getten, an' they will'nt sell me no less than hawf an ounce at t'public yonder. Now don't be hard maister, for I'm itching for a smoke. I met a chap i t'road just now, an' he says to me, "Its a day i' a hundred", says he.

"Mebbe", says I, "for them as hes loving friends an a pipe o' baccy!"

He never varies his even flow of voice, and the half penny still looks at me from his extended palm. It is masterly and I hand him my pouch without a protest.

"Pocket your halfpenny and fill up," I mutter.

He is an artist. He shows no haste in restoring the coin to the pocket with the gaping seams; nay, he even presses me to accept the money, and withdraws at at last with a regretful air. A silence follows, and he looks up from filling his pipe to find me smiling broadly at him. I think that he sees in me a touch of nature that makes us kin, for he, too, lets the half of a smile wrinkle his mouth corners.

"I'll give you a shilling, if you'll tell me something? I hazard.

"A shillin's a lot o' brass, what is it maister?"

"I want to know how often that half penny has filled you pipe for you. Come, fairly now – how often?"

"Well – twenty times since yesterday so far as I can reckon up. But, maister," he adds, leaning confidentially towards me as the shilling changes hands, – "if ever ye think o' tryin' that game, keep clear o' Lancashire. I once tried it on a chap fro' Lancashire an' I lost mi ha'penny".

Burnsall Church [22]

Burnsall Church, whose noble tower adds interest to the vale is a magnificent structure, originally built in the Norman style. It is dedicated to St Wilfred, the patron saint of Ripon. It was repaired at the expense of Sir William Craven, "Knight and Alderman of ye citie of London in 1612." In 1857-8 the church underwent a complete restoration.

"Many characteristic stories are told of the Rev. John Alcock, who was rector at Burnsall, and died there in the year 1810. When Peter Riley was sexton of

Burnsall, he and the parson were, one wild wintry day, the only persons present at the sunday morning service. But the good rector went through the service notwithstanding; and when he commenced with the usual words – "Dearly beloved brethren" – the listening sexton suddenly started up and called out – "Neea, [*nay*] Neea; ye maun't say 'Dearly beloved brethren' ye maun [*must*] say – Dearly beloved Pete."

Burnsall Grammar School [23]

Adjoining the churchyard is the old Grammar School, founded in 1603 [02] by Sir William Craven. He also endowed the school, which has always been noted for its high class education. At a time when Parson Alcock was master of the school as well as rector, Eugene Aram was one of the pupils. *Eugene Aram was one of four fraudsters in Knaresborough in 1744 who fell out with the result that he murdered one of the others for which he was hanged at York in 1759.* The original building, of which we here have a view is still standing, an excellent example of the domestic style of that age. The beautiful old leaded window panes are very characteristic. The school maintains the good traditions of the founder and is still attended by a number of boys and girls daily. *Still in use as a school.*

Burnsall Bridge [24]

Resuming our ramble, we follow the path close to the river, which here abounds with grayling and trout. It is no wonder that among anglers Burnsall is a favourite resort.

"Here by the stream,
Waltonians dream;
Or ply their craft
assiduously,
With mimic fly, tempt
wanton fry,
And hook them, aye,
right warily."

Burnsall from the north [25]

Presently we arrive at a most delightful spot known as Loup Scar, - Here the river forms a sort of a bend in the shape of a shepherds crook, on account of its course being suddenly turned by a great mass of limestone rock, connected at some time with a still bolder mass on the other side.

Hebden Swing Bridge

[26]

Hebden swing bridge and stepping stones. We cross by the bridge in order to take a peep at the old village, and also take a scramble up the wild and rocky Hebden Gill.

27

Waterwheel. Hebden [27]

This large waterwheel at Hebden is in connection with the working of the old lead mines high up on the moors and was used for the purpose of drawing off water from the mines. It will be about 50 years ago [*i.e. 1850s*] since it ceased working. *It has long since disappeared.*

Hebden Village [28]

Hebden village takes its name from its situation, High Dene, the deep valley running into the Wharfe from the lofty ridges which separate Netherdale from Craven. Many a story of old 'characters' and past events which make up the life of the village in the olden times might be recounted did time permit. But we cannot pass without recounting a little occurence in connection with old Henry Baines, a staunch Wesleyan. Poor old Henry he had to seek relief in the end from the Parish authorities, and when they came to arrange the allowance, he wagged his tongue loud and long in support of his contention that he had kept off parish relief "till he wor ommost ready to deaa!" They asked him to sign his name in the book provided for that purpose.

"Nay," he said, "I nivver put my name o'paper i' all may deays."

"Well then," came the request, "You must make a cross, Henry."

"A cross," ejaculated the old man, "Aw'll noan turn roman catholic for all t'brass i t'world, aw'll deaa first."

Hole Bottom Farm [29]

Above Scala waterfall in Hebden Gill is Hole Bottom Farm. Its name is very appropriate, for the hills rise above it on every hand. Here dwelt the Bowdins. The family were famous musicians. The seven brothers, Henry, Thomas, Dick, Orlando, Horatio, Augustine, and Daniel, with their father, were an orchestra in themselves.

The Falling Cliff. (Hebden Gill) [30]

Away to our right, on the top of the scar, is seen "The Falling Cliff", which has detached itself from the main headland, and seems ready to come crashing down into the valley below. The old men of the dale, declare that the rock moves an inch or two every year. *It did finally collapse in 1941.*

Grassington Low Mill and Stepping Stones [31]

Returning once more to the banks of the Wharfe, we are soon by the Grassington Low Mills and stepping stones. *Originally a corn mill this was at that time a textile mill, and after varied uses is now residential.*

Linton Church (from the river) [32]

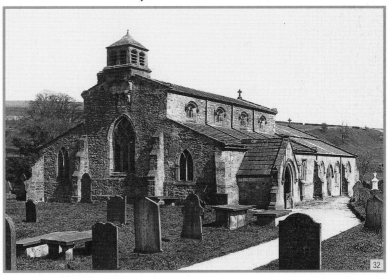

The name "Linton" derives from flax once grown there. A view of Linton Church, which stands in a most secluded situation on a bend in the Wharfe. Its style of architecture originally was Norman, but there may have been a Saxon edifice previous to the Norman period. The Norman building dated from 1150, or, thereabouts. The Norman belfry, which the church possesses is one of the few remaining in England, and gives it quite a continental appearance. In 1733 to 1776, Benjamin Smith, B.D. and nephew of Sir Isaac Newton, was Rector at Linton.

A short time ago I spent the whole of one day lounging about here opposite the old church; and witnessed the coming to the sacred edifice on the morning - a wedding party, all gay and joyous; at noon a solemn procession bearing to its last long rest the remains of a dear and long respected old dales-woman; and a little later, a small group, full of hope and joy for the future, bringing a babe to christen.

A commercial traveller, staying the weekend with some friends, had always had a disliking to go to church or chapel in the evening, as he was in the habit of falling asleep during the sermon. Eventually some of the young ladies where he was staying persuaded him to go. As usual, he went into a deep slumber as the discourse was proceeding. Before concluding, the parson asked all who would like to go to heaven to stand up. Everybody uprose except the traveller. His lady friends woke him up, however. The preacher then asked those to stand up who would like to go to the other place, and the traveller, after rubbing his eyes, stood up and found he was the only one so doing. He gazed up at the pulpit and exclaimed, – "Well parson, I don't know what you're voting for, but there's only you and me stood up."

Linton Falls in flood [33]

[*Old bridge*] The most favourable time to see the falls is, of course, when the river is flooded; then the scene is awfully grand, far too grand for my feeble words to describe. *"Awfully" here being used in its original sense: "full of awe"*.

The old "tin" bridge [34]

The bridge in slide 33 being removed in 1904 to be replaced by the one seen in slide 35, This survived until it was itself replaced in 1989 by one in wood built by the army.

Linton Falls

[35]

[New bridge] Linton Falls, one of the grandest rock-and-water scenes on the Wharfe. Here the rocks are bold in character, and the cascades are numerous; the water dashes down into the seething boiling cauldrons, sending its spray in all directions.

I have stood on the bridge when the water has come rushing down with a thundering roar,

hurling itself with mighty force over the rocks, and sending forth grey clouds of spray and foam, greatly adding to the effect, and making a picture wild and weird in the extreme.

View from the Bridge. (Greenhaw House) [36]

Here we have a view taken from the bridge, with Gudgeon House, now called Greenhaw House, in the background. *A note below the mounted print of the slide states "I made this my home*  *when visiting Linton".* The scenery of the Wharfe at Linton is very charming, and the waterfalls are one of the sights of the neighbourhood.

Threshfield Grammar School [37]

Threshfield Grammar School is an ancient looking place, situate half-a-mile from Grassington, Linton, and Threshfield. It serves a wide district. The endowment was by the Rev. Matthew Hewitt, a former rector of Linton, and of whom there is a memorial in Linton Church. He died in 1674. Among an earlier race of pupils who received the rudiments of their education here was the great Dr Whittaker, the Craven historian. Dr Dodgson, and Dr William Craven. The Rev.

Mr Sheepshanks, with whose family Sheepshanks, Astronomer Royal, was connected, was one of the former masters of the school.

The building remains unchanged as a school.

Troutbeck House (Linton) [38]

The house at Linton called "Troutbeck" at present the residence of Mr Halliwell Sutcliffe, novelist, *[1870-1932]* was formerly known as "White Abbey".

Note woman sitting in front of house to left. This is still a private house and has reverted to the name "White Abbey".

Grassington Bridge [39]

Grassington Bridge is a very fine stone structure, and the views both up and down the river are very fine indeed. We are now very near to Grassington Railway Station, which bears the significant name of the Yorkshire Dales Railway it was opened on July 30th 1902. *This ran from Skipton and was closed to passenger traffic in 1930.* To our right are the beautiful Grass Woods.

Grassington Old Hall [40]

Claimed to be the oldest inhabited house in Craven. *Parts date back to the 13th century and it is probably the site of the original*

manor house. It remains a private house behind high walls to the west of the square.

The Village Smithy (Grassington) [41]

The village smithy which stands at the entrance to the market square. It was here where Tom Lee [*murderer, see below*], along with his apprentice Jack Sharp, spent his working days. *With the decline in the use of horses this became a greengrocers; it now sells woodcrafts. Another smithy turned art gallery above the market square is now said to be that of Tom Lee.*

42

The Market Place (Grassington) [42]

Trees now bigger; the hotel at the top of the market square is now a "Country Concept" boutique. Grassington Market Square, where the celebrated fairs were held. Bull baiting was greatly practised at Grassington in former times, and the scenes of blood and revelry were witnessed by people of all classes in large numbers. Badger baiting was also a favourite sport, and continued long after Bull baiting had been forbidden by law. Also many ancient and innocent pastimes were practised, such as – Treacle eating, mumming, sword-dancing, Riding the stang [*a demonstration against wife-beaters*], Clock dressing, &c Shrovetide was a noticeable time, the customs of the week being varied from the general order of things in other places. There was Collop-Monday, Fritter-Tuesday, Pancake-Wednesday, and Lousy-Thursday. On Monday they cut their first rashers of home fed bacon; on Tuesday they partook of fritters, rich and toothsome, as more befitting the festive character of the day than pancakes, and children went from door to door collecting them, say[*ing*] at each house – "Pray now a Fruttah." On Wednesday they came down to pancakes, as harmonising with the humility and penitence required on the first day of Lent, and on Thursday it was "every lad catch his lass and kiss her" to escape the penalty of being called Lousy all the year. It was woebetide the girl who ventured out upon it. Among the chief features were the annual processions of the various clubs. The Miners Club. The Oddfellows Club. The Foresters Club and others. These were generally headed by the –

Grassington Brass Band [43]

"The Duke's Own" as it was called, in showy uniform. (This is a copy from an old print taken about 50 years ago.) [*c.1850 labelled "amature", see drum*] Among the bandsmen were Wiseman the noted Cornet player; Joseph Hodgson, master of the Clarionet; and William Latham the champion Trombonist. The Drummer was Jack Slack, whose facial contortions kept time to the music to the amusement of everybody. He was a man overflowing with wit and humour. It was a rule to give half-a-crown to each of the members to spend in drink at the annual festival, but those who got drunk were fined five shillings, as a great number of them did this, the club made more by the fines than they lost by the gifts.[!]

Main street Grassington [44]

This shows the bottom of the main street Grassington where the horse omnibuses up the dale start. *Already in the 1950s the Commercial Inn had become Barclays Bank and the stone roof had been replaced by slate.*

Entering the Lower Grass Woods by the style near the river we come to a long deep pool named - - -

Lang Dub (Grass Woods) [45]

Shadowed by graceful beaches and other trees. Here the water is very still.

Grasswoods and the river banks hereabouts is a delightful spot. A very fairyland around us, richly carpeted with flowers of varied hue, and the air redolent with their rich fragrance. The suspension bridge which belongs to Netherside Hall is private. *It is no longer there.*

Netherside Hall (from Grass Woods) [46]

The Beautiful Hall is embossed in luxuriant leafage, and is in a most romantic position, reared high up on the Crag above the magnificent stretch of forest that descends precipitously to the edge of the river. *The trees are now so tall that only the roof of the hall is visible. On the left bank (opposite the hall) trees aged say 70 years among old tree stumps indicate woodland management. This is now a schools residential centre for North Yorkshire Council.*

Front of Netherside Hall [47]

This magnificent mansion was built at great cost by the Nowells. And is at present owned by Colonel Nowell. John Broughton, the old Grassington Poet, tells us –

"That this extensive structure of gothic kind,
from its numerous train of chimnies, it would appear,
contained as many rooms, as are weeks in a year".

Long view of Wharfe near Netherside [48]

The Grass Woods Murder [*1766 abridged*] You cannot expect to visit Grassington and Grass Woods without hearing something of the foul and brutal murder of Dr Petty. You learn how Tom Lee, a blacksmith and landlord of the Blue Anchor, a man of ill repute, had got himself into the power of the village doctor through having visited him time after time to have his wounds dressed, the results of dubious midnight exploits. How at the Anglers Arms at Kilnsey the doctor used his influence over the blacksmith, to end a quarrel between him and Dick Mytton, another blacksmith, from Littondale. [*Mittons still farmed in the Dale in the 1940s.*] How Tom Lee left the inn breathing dark vengeance, and how the doctor failed to return home that night, or the next, or ever.

In the dead of night a lonely horseman approaches the wood, and bends down to, open the rustic gate, a hurried blow with a hedgestake lays him in the grass; a short sharp struggle in the dank weeds; a glistening knife; a riderless horse galloping homewards; a stealthy figure dragging a loathsome burden into the lonely wood; a horror-stricken blacksmith stealing home, but to reveal to his waiting wife the guilty crime, only to be overheard by his listening apprentice Jack Sharp. How in order to close Jack's mouth the pair go forth with pick and spade, and finding some lingering spark of life in the unfortunate doctor, the blacksmith makes the apprentice drive the knife home and finish the foul deed.

Looking up the Dale (from Dew bottom scar) [49]

Making our way through the wood to the northern point of Dew bottom scar we have one of the grandest and most extensive views in Upper Wharfedale. Kilnsey Crag juts prominently into view, with Hawkswick Clowder and the wild moors of Littondale rising beyond. Northward towers Buckden Gable. The villages of Kilnsey, Coniston, and Kettlewell, nestle in the bosom of the valley, while stretching away for miles the silvery Wharfe is eventually lost in the maze of the distance.

The horse omnibus (and mail carrier) rattling along in a cloud of dust through Grass Woods [50]

The driver was Harry Stubbs whose grandson in the 1950s kept a pub in Grassington.
The poem "The Highwayman" by Alfred Noyes has a phrase:
"The white road smoking behind him".

Conistone (looking towards Kilnsey) [51]

Leaving Grassington by the highway through the woods a three miles tramp brings us to Conistone, – or King's town, as its name signifies. In the distance we have a grand view of Kilnsey and to the right – Kilnsey Crag. *The maypole has long-since gone.*

Conistone Church [52]

The old Norman Church is a gem of antiquity, going back to the last years of the conqueror. Until 1846 it was without a chancel.

This has two Saxon arches and is probably the oldest church in Craven. It was restored in 1958 when electric light and central heating were installed.

Old White-washed cottage (Conistone)

[53]

A Conistone homestead. A typical yeoman's dwelling. At one time Conistone was noted for its Whangby cheese, which

was so tough that it often needed a hatchet to cut it.

Kilnsey (sheep) [54]

The Hamlet of Kilnsey overshadowed by its beetling [*overhanging*] rock is on the other side of the Wharfe. Kilnsey in monastic times belonged to Fountains Abbey - [*it was a "Grange"*]. The annual sheep washing and shearing, to the accompaniment of the bleatings of a vast multitude of sheep was the great event of the year in the hey-days of the monastery. After washing and clipping, the wool was conveyed on wains by various old roads over the Fells to Fountains Abbey. *The nearer inn is the Anglers Inn and the further one the Tennants Arms and only the latter remains as an inn (with the same name). This photograph was used as Figure 9.3 in* Sheep and Man *by M. L. Ryder (Duckworth, 1983) where the sheep were likened to Masham crosses.*

Kilnsey Old Hall (near view) [55]

The monks have left their impress of occupation here, judging from the remains of rich frescoes in the Old Hall, which is now used as a mistle [*cow house*] and barn; traces of this connection remain in a remarkable frieze, which extends round one of the rooms, the carved emblems being religious and ecclesiastical. Angels, roses, lilies, vines, oak leaves, and acorns appear in great perfection. It is remarkable that such an example of wall decoration should be found in such

55

an unlooked for place.

The Hall was originally enclosed within a courtyard and approached through two large archways. But the whole of these are now gone. Over one of the entrances are the initials and date C. W. 1648, no doubt indicating the builder of the house, Christopher Wade, whose son Cuthbert Wade, was a captain in the Royalist forces during the civil war. *The hall, a listed building, was in 2001 renovated as a private house and bed and breakfast accommodation.*

Kilnsey Crag [56]

This vast mass of limestone extends by the highway for nearly half-a-mile, and is nearly 200 feet high, while in one place it leans over 40 feet. It is one of the wonders of Yorkshire; its general bareness is beautifully relieved in places by ivy, fern, and wood. It is the secure haunt of numberless jackdaws, swallows and numerous other birds. *I remember the birds in the 1940s, but the crag is now the perpetual haunt of rock climbers.*

Some have supposed this to be an ancient sea-cliff, and ages ago the waves of an inland sea lashed this, and several maritime plants still grow wild within the vicinity. *In fact it was shaped by a galcier during the Ice Ages.* Although appearing so near the highway, it requires the energies of a good thrower to hit it with a stone. *It appears so near that people think that they can throw a stone as far as the rock, but I doubt whether it is possible.*

Taking leave of Kilnsey Crag, we push forward and are soon at the point where Wharfedale divides into two branches; known respectively as Kettlewelldale and Littondale. The Wharfe traverses the district of Kettlewelldale and the river Skirfare runs through Littondale, formerly called 'Amerdale'. Bidding a temporary adieu to the Wharfe we proceed up the vale of the Skirfare.

The first hamlet we come to is Hawkswick; it is composed principally of farmsteads and is delightfully situated on the river's bank, - nestling beneath a hill. The bridge at Hawkswick has several times been swept away by floods, and appears destined to [*experience*] that fate again.

56

Jacky Allan (on broom stick) [57]

His morning exercise. Passing through the village a short time ago I took a snap-shot of this young gentleman just starting out for a morning's canter on his (mother's) sweeping charger.

Looking up Littondale (from Arncliffe) [58]

From the 'Eagles Cliff', formerly a favourite resort of eagles, and where that large and fierce bird of prey is said in ancient times to

have built his eyrie, we obtain an uninterrupted view of a greater part of Littondale. Looking up the vale of the Skirfare we can note its many windings, until we can see very little of it. The dale head is enclosed with lofty fells, and

about Halton Gill is so shut in there appears no visible outlet. About halfway between Arncliffe and Litton, is 'Scoska' Cave, locally known as 'Gilders bank'. The entrance is imposing and can be seen on the south west side of the valley. *Charles Kingsley used to visit a house in this village while he was writing the* Water Babies.

Arncliffe Church [59]

Arncliffe church [*of St Oswald*] was rebuilt in the reign of Henry VIII, and underwent a complete restoration in 1832. *In fact in 1841 on Norman foundations and retaining the 15th century tower.*

Owl Cotes (Arncliffe) [60]

Slide labelled "Old", which is deleted and replaced by "Owl" in text. In passing 'Owl Cotes', on our way up the dale we cannot but pause a moment to admire the old homestead by the side of the highway, with its old walls covered with ivy, its leaves glistening in the sunshine, its old fashioned windows, outstanding doorway and romantic surroundings. These rustic homesteads, here and there, still retain features which combine to form one of the most charming pictures of a rural village. *This is still a private house named OLD Cotes (and Old Cote Farm), with the date 1690 and the initials S.M.S. over the door.*

Gildersbank Cave (Littondale) [61]

'Scoska', or 'Gildersbank Cave', is seen up the side of a rocky slope, 1000 feet above sea level, and 250 feet above the river Skirfare. Partly covered with stunted trees. In wet seasons a stream trinkles out of the cave and falls in a series of small cascades, and finds its way to the river below. It was in this cave that the skull and other bones of a female Celt were found, quite recently, (1906) by members of the Yorkshire Ramblers Club. *Pasted on the opposite page is a press cutting from the* Yorkshire Daily Observer *dated March 15, 1906, describing the discovery. The next page has a similar cutting from the* Leeds Mercury *dated June 15, 1906.*

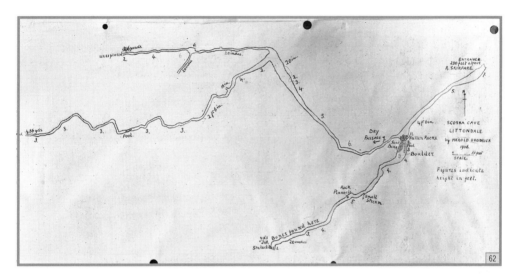

Plan of Scoska Cave [62]

About 45 yards from the entrance the cave expands into a small chamber, the main branch continuing to the right. On the left hand side of the chamber is another branch, which is entered by creeping under a low ledge of rock about 18 inches high, the floor being covered with loose stones, with here and there pools of water. Following this latter passage, in a very few yards the roof rises, and it is again possible to stand erect. Proceeding, the roof becomes lower and lower, until progress is only possible by creeping along the course of a small stream. The bones were found in this cramped passage, the roof being scarcely two feet high, and in some places bristling with stalactites, many of which had to be broken to afford a passage, which goes to prove that this part of the cave had been undisturbed for centuries.

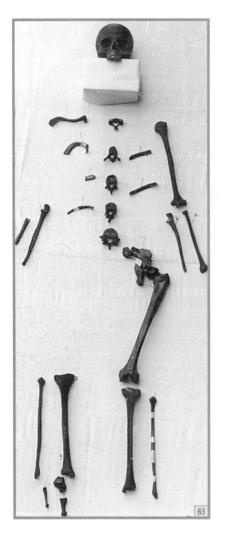

63

Skeleton of Female Celt [63]

The remains were submitted to Prof. Boyd Dawkins, *[Sir William Boyd Dawkins (1837-1929) professor of geology at Manchester University]* a famous authority, who has had much to do with cave excavations in this country, and he promptly pronounced them to be those of a woman belonging to the Goidelic section of the Celtic race.

It is probable that she lived towards the termination of the Bronze Age. So that the bones were presumably quite 2000 years old. *Today we consider that the Bronze Age ended about 750 BC and that the Celts belonged to the succeeding Iron Age.*

It is calculated that she would be about 5 ft 3 ins in height, and about 40 years of age at the time of her death.

A description of the skeleton by C. A. Hill appeared in the Journal of Anatomy and Physiology *vol. 41, pp. 221-230 (1907) but considerable enquiry among specialists in this field today has failed to unearth any more recent research on the skeleton, e.g. dating by modern methods.*

The Queen's Arms (Litton) [64]

The 'Queen's Arms' a very comfortable and popular tourists quarters. [*Note use of term "tourist" at that date.*] Recently fit up with every modern convenience for the comfort of visitors. On my recommendation some time ago a party of ladies and gentlemen (friends of mine) spent a week's holiday up the dale at a lonely farm high up on the hill side miles away from everywhere. Unfortunately the weather was against them; for it rained, and rained, and rained; and when it rains up the dale - it rains. For about three days it rained morning, noon, and eve, consequently their boots and feet got very wet, so one of the young men suggested greasing their boots with Castor oil, in order to make them waterproof; as they had no Castor oil at the farm, a messenger (one of the farm hands,) was despatched, on horseback to the nearest village store, for half a pound, - some

five or six miles distant. But they never told him what they wanted it for. Just as the party were sitting down to lunch, the messenger returned, having been away all morning. "Well, George," said one of the gentlemen, "did you get the Castor oil?" "No sir," replied George, Mr Jefferson said as he had no Castor oil in at present so he sent you a box of Beecham Pills, instead, saying as you would perhaps manage until the Castor oil arrived". They simply roared with laughter when George had retired, especially the ladies. The pills were shared round, however, and by appearances next morning had been made good use of.

65

Post Office, Litton, The Village Tailor [65]

Litton Post office. Drapery stores. Sweets and Tobacco. Tailor. Lemonade and Stone Ginger &c. Mr Battersby, Post master general & village tailor. Mrs Battersby could not be induced to stand for her photograph. She disappeared inside the doorway, saying "Neaa, I's too plain looking to be photographed, I's too short and fat, I sud look too much like a sack o' flour wi a string tied roond t'middle." *The telegraph service reached Litton in 1905.*

Foxup (Head of Littondale) [66]

About half-a-mile beyond Halton Gill church we have Foxup. The dale head appears so shut in with lofty fells that there appears no visible outlet. From Halton Gill there is a fine mountain walk over Horse-head Pass to Raisgill in Langstrothdale. An old pack-horse route in fact, and one of the highest in

Yorkshire. The summit nearly 2000 feet high commands one of the very finest views to be had among the upper western ranges. From no point in our district are the chief Yorkshire mountains more admirably or more picturesquely grouped. From nowhere do we see a wilder, bolder, or more striking assemblage of gaunt and solitary hills than from the summit of this now almost unknown and little frequented pass.

Kettlewell (from the south) [67]

Resuming the course of the wharfe - the view of Kettlewell from the Kilnsey road on this side of the valley is very fine, showing the whole of the town with terraced scars and the gaunt form of Great Whernside towering beyond. *There is now a petrol filling station in the foreground.*

"Blue Bell" and "Race Horses" (Kettlewell) [68]

The two inns still have the same names. Kettlewell is six miles from Grassington, and previous to the advent of the Yorkshire Dales railway was further from a railway station than any town in England. It is a delightful place to stay at. The hotel accommodation is plain but good, of the old fashioned inn sort. In respect both of itself and its inns there is no cleaner village in England.

While seated in a village Inn eating lunch one day, at a time when Partridge was not in season, a police inspector, in plain clothes walked in and seated himself at the table.

"Waiter, bring me Partridge".

"Yes, sir."

The dinner was brought, and eaten, when he called again,

"Waiter, ask the Boss to step this way."

"Yes, sir; What for sir?"

"Well I'm a police inspector, and I want to inform him that he will have to appear before the magistrate for selling Partridge out of season".

"You didnt have Partridge, sir." "I didnt, then what was it then?"

"It was Crow, sir."

That poor inspector, you should have seen his jaw drop, and his stomach heave.

May Pole and Village Green (Kettlewell) [69]

The district does not perhaps possess the sylvan beauties of the lower dale, yet the grouping of its white-washed cottages, thrown into all conceivable shapes, by the brink of the rivulet toned with age or musty with long centuries of wear. - - - Surrounded by ranges of stern hills, [which] shed a halo and charm of beauty on an otherwise sterile region. *There is no longer a village green, but the maypole is still there, with the ring of stones and three seats.*

Cutliffe Hine's House (Kettlewell) [70]

Here we have the residence of Mr Cutliffe Hine [Hyne], novelist, and author of "The adventures of Captain Kettle" &c - *He bought the house in 1901 and died there in 1944, being buried in Kettlewell churchyard. His daughter Miss Mildred Nancy Cutliffe-Hyne lived in the house until dying there on 26 December 1999 aged 97.*

Man with Milking-can [71]

Far from the maddening crowd, this grey, quiet, self contained little village, is a convenient centre for all round excursions. It is the axis of a wheel, with a track of some sort forming its spokes in all directions. The aspiring climber, too, may easily reach the top of Great Whernside, or Buckden Pike, or even Penyghent. No where in the dale is the grand massive limestone scar so finely evidenced as it is here. *Milk was still carried home on the back like this in the 1950s and may still be done.*

The old Hall, Kettlewell

[72]

This is still a private house in Leyburn Road.

The Beck (Kettlewell)

[73]

One striking feature of Kettlewell which one sees and hears almost at every turn is water. It comes swirling from ravines in the hills, leaping and bubbling under bridges and over

boulders, washing the walls of the houses in its madcap rush to the river.

Mr Jaques (Sexton. Kettlewell) [74]

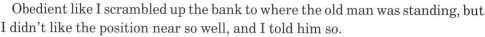

My old friend Jaques. 36 years Sexton, and 52 years Bell ringer.

While engaged in photographing this view [*see slide 73*] I was startled by a voice from behind. "Nah then! whats tha up tul dahn there?"

Turning round I beheld a cheerful looking old dale's-man leaning on his stick; "Just taking a photograph, sir, thats' all;"

"Haw! so that's thi game is it? Well cum up here, then, this is t'best place ta tak bridge from."

Obedient like I scrambled up the bank to where the old man was standing, but I didn't like the position near so well, and I told him so.

"I'se tellin' thi", shouted the old man, "this is t'best place i'all t'wurld to tak t'view from; bless thi I owt ta knaw, I lived here afoor thi faather wor born, an' I've seen many a hundred tak it froo here."

"Indeed", I said, "well, now that being the case I wouldn't take one from there on any account."

"Noo then", returned the old man when he saw that I had finished, "is thoo bahn to strike t'owd man afoor thoo goes?"

"Strike — what?" replied I, "no sir, your mistaken, I'm no fighting man."

"Noa, tha dosn't comphrend, I mean is thoo bahn ta tak t'owd man's likeness?"

"Oh, I see, you want me to take a photograph of you; why of course I will with the greatest of pleasure".

After taking his photograph I enquired to what address I could post him a copy.

"Jaques. Sexton. Kettlewell. Via Skipton" promptly came the reply.

"Oh, indeed; thank you Mr Jaques, delighted to make your aquaintance, then you're Sexton are you?"

"Yes of course I is, what else dus ta think I cud be, I'se bin Sexton for 36 years, an t bell ringer 52 years. I hed an accident some time since, - tha sees I wor ringing one day as usual, an' sum hah t'rope gat entangled rahnd my feet an' I fell an' brak one o' mi legs, an' nah tha sees I'se a bit lame, an' hes ta gan aboot wi a stick."

"Very sad," I said, and sympathised with the old gentleman.

"Yes!" he went on, "I wor t'leader o' t' band here for 46 years, I started leading when I wor nobbut 15 years owd."

"Wonderful", I said; - "Are you married?" I ventured, thinking to gain a little knowledge of his home life.

"Of course I is, Ise bin wed 47 years; I'se 9 children living, t'owdest is 46, an' youngest is 24."

"And how many grand children have you," I enquired.

Here the old sexton straightened himself up, stared at me a moment, and then in an enquiring tone of voice said, - "Now what thoo putting dahn i' that there fancy pocket book o' thine? its taking thee a fearsome time to write my name and address; but I'se thinkin' I'se given thee sum news. Just thee put that book an' pencil i thi pocket or else we sall pairt company. I know I'se a little bit frisky this morn'; it wor t fair day yester, an' I gat a little drop too much to drink; didn't tha noatice hah mi eyes sparkled?"

"No," I said, I had not noticed any sparkling, but I said that I thought he was a very jovial sort of man. He then asked me if ever I had been inside the old church.

"Yes, I had a long time ago." I said, "but I should be delighted to go in again."

"Well then, sam up thi traps, mi lad, and cum on."

I went and spent a very pleasant hour, he showed me many interesting things, and told me many droll stories relating to his work as Sexton at Kettlewell church.

In the Mss there is a cutting from the Yorkshire Evening Post *dated 30 March 1911 reporting the Golden Wedding of Mr and Mrs Jaques and stating that he had been a bell-ringer for 59 years - the 52 years therefore refers to 1904. They were married on Easter Saturday 1861. When I published this photo in* The Dalesman *during the 1950s I had a letter from his granddaughter who was a farmers wife in Hawes. A grandson name Olly Jacques was a farmer in Grassington.*

Kettlewell church [75]

The old Norman church of Kettlewell was removed in 1820, and the present neat structure, built of Whernside grit, erected on its site as recently as 1885. *Only the 12th Century "tub" font remains.*

Inside Douk Cave (Looking out) [76]

The exploration of Douk Cave is somewhat difficult, and from the very rugged, wet, and rocky nature of the channels not without danger. The cavern is of great extent, and has several lateral passages of great length. The footway is very rough and the explorer must be prepared for a good wetting, as the passage, - always lofty enough to permit of walking erect, runs along the rocky bed of the stream, which penetrates its whole length. This view I took from inside the cave looking out.

Summit of Great Whernside [77]

It is three miles from the village [*of Kettlewell*] to the summit of Great Whernside, which hereabouts is strewn with huge masses of rock, piled around in great confusion. *The caption of his print gives the height as 2310 ft.*

When the hot sun shines on limestone fell and scar, the white road [*Macadam but not tarred*] up the dale will gladly be exchanged for the pleasanter path through the grassy meadows along the river's bank to snug little Starbotton at the foot of Cam Gill.

Starbotton (Fell side)

[78]

Behind there on the fell side, two hundred years ago, the waters burst at flood-time, ran upward in a liquid pillar and fell with a crash that wrecked the village. It is Starbotton's only history and it would have been happier for the lack of it. Never perhaps in recent centuries has the locality been better entitled to the description of "stony bottom", [*this is thought to be the origin of the name*] than after that historic flood mentioned, as having ruined this prosperous dale village in the year 1686. Many of the inhabitants perished, and many head of cattle and sheep were drowned. The ancient streams were diverted and several bridges were driven down, and overwhelmed, and many houses were destroyed.

Rustic Cottage (Marshall's Starbotton) [79]

Not all the houses were washed away, although some of them we are told were filled with gravel up to the chamber windows. The whole place has a primitive appearance, with many picturesque cottages. *After being a shop and PO this is again a house named "Post House" still with the stone canopy.*

Fox and Hounds (Starbotton)

[80]

'Ye olde Inn' is a typical picture of the past. *The name is still the same.*

Buckden [81]

The extensive woods and Buckden Park belonging to the Crompton-Stansfield family add in no small degree to the beauty of the surroundings, and help to relieve the bareness of the overhanging hills, where deer still roam at pleasure. The deer that gave the village its name, browse yet-in lessening numbers on the hill slopes. *Some of these woods were felled at the end of World War II. By that*

time few, if any, deer remained; today much of the area around Buckden, and extending up Langstrothdale, belongs to the National Trust.

Wesleyan Chapel (Buckden) [82]

Date above the door 1891. The most northerly Chapel in the Grassington circuit, is the small Wesleyan Chapel at Buckden, standing very picturesquely beneath a wild range of stone-fenced hills. *This was closed during World War II, but was in use again in 1995; by 1997 it had been converted to two houses. He does not say that the large building to the right is the back of Buckden House, then the home of the Crompton-Stansfield family, where I was evacuated with Leeds Grammar School during 1941. During the 1950s it was a Methodist Guild Home. It is now an outdoor pursuits centre of Bradford Education Department. During August 1995 hay was still being raked by hand in the steep fields behind the village.*

Visitors to this wild and beautiful part of Wharfedale, should not fail to visit the romantic neighbourhood of Cray, where are some very fine waterfalls. On our left a picturesque waterfall with three or four long leaps widening to their base, "comes of the darksome haggs and shaws with much cadence". Leaving its craggy little amphitheatre, it hurries onward a commonplace gill, which quite belies its pretensions of a few moments ago, and wimples beneath the road bridge. *A 1940s walk from Buckden to Cray followed what was said to be a Roman road through Rakes Wood on the slopes of Buckden Pike.*

Waterfall (to right of road) [83]

Author to left, C. Mellor to right. To our right another stream has worn a passage through the craggs, making first a bold leap, then two cascades, but, looking beyond, up a gap in the fell side, it can be seen coming for nearly half-a-mile.

Cray village [84]

Leaving the road we pass behind the tiny hamlet of Cray, and enter Cray Gill. In summer a most delightful region.

Hubberholme Church [85]

Hubberholme is one of the oldest places in Upper Wharfedale. Its church, which is dedicated to St Michael, stands in one of the most remote spots for a place of worship now existing in England. The situation is exceedingly picturesque; its time-stained walls and low square [*Norman*] tower being in admirable harmony

with the surroundings. *By the 1940s there were yew trees on each side of the door, which by 1997 were stumps, but there are two yews on the right of the path when approaching the door.*

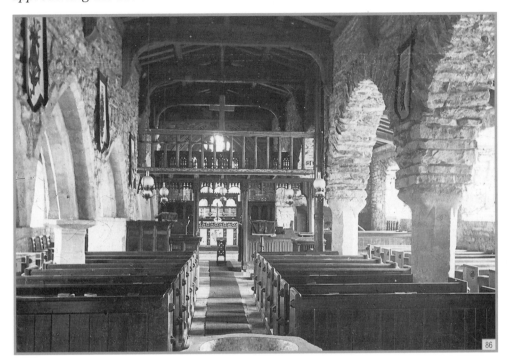

Interior Hubberholme Church [86]

The foundation is of high antiquity, the first church here probably having been destroyed by the Danes. The interior is one of the quaintest and most remarkable to be found in Yorkshire; with its ancient rood loft and rough stone arches. The ancient rood, or image of Christ on the cross, has however, disappeared, and in its place is the present plain cross, erected nearly 50 years ago. [1850s] The masonry of the walls and some of the arches is extremely crude. *These coats of arms are no longer displayed and by the 1940s the pews had been replaced by oak ones carved by Robert Thompson of Kilburn, whose trade-mark was a carved mouse.* But the most striking feature of the interesting interior, happily retained, is the original 16th century Rood-loft, separating the Choir from the body of the church.

16th Century Rood-loft (or screen) [87]

Few of these symbolic erections remain in England, nor are any, I believe, known to be of an earlier date than the 16th century. The Hubberholme rood-screen is therefore of very special interest and fortunately retains its original character

almost entire. On it there is a short inscription and date, - "built 1558 William Jake, carpenter." This was the year when Queen Mary died, and the Protestant Elizabeth ascended the throne, and the use of such objects was prohibited.

Bridge and George Inn [88]

Leaving the church we cross the bridge - which divides Hubberholme from Kirkgill, where stands the last house of call between Hubberholme

and Wensleydale; and Hubberholme and Ribblesdale. This little 'public' is typical of the dales; a quite and peaceful homestead which for many years served for the parsonage at Hubberholme. Metaphorically speaking, we shall have to go round to the back, to get to the front of this house. *During the 1950s it was still owned by the church and was/is famous for the annual letting of a pasture, the rent of which goes to the poor, held there each January.*

George Inn (Kirkgill, sheep) [89]

The George Inn stands with its back to the highroad, while its door and windows are placed modestly at the rear side, from which circumstance this house is not recognised as an Inn. *The obviously new part at the end has been further altered to provide accommodation for the landlord.*

George Inn (Kirkgill, Grace Pawson) [90]

But let us take a peep inside the old Inn, and have a little chat with the good old dame Grace Pawson, an elderly maiden, with colourless hair, - and called Grace by all the company present. Here we see Grace washing out the milk pails, for you must know that Grace keeps Cows, and also pigs, Ducks, Geese, and Poultry, quite a little farm, in fact, - to attend to, in addition to looking after the quaint old Inn. *She disliked being photographed and died in 1925, the last of her family to keep the inn. She was 79 and is buried in Hubberholme churchyard.*

Grace driving cattle to pastures [91]

Langsettle George Inn (Kirkgill)

[92]

But step inside, you are very welcome and feel at home almost before you cross the threshold. The place is perfection of 'Ye olde Inn' of bygone days, and in its way quite unique. The old oak Langsettle is black with age; how long it has been in the family Grace could not tell; hundreds of years perhaps. It is a cherished heirloom, and money would not tempt Grace to part with it. *Note the shelves behind each step of the stairs on which are candlesticks and slippers. The interior had changed by the 1950s when it was possible to stay there for the first time since the 1930s (and I did so) - the steep stairs had gone but the fireplace surround was still there in 1997.*

Interior George Inn (Delft-rack) [93]

On the side near the door is an ancient dresser; also a delft-rack on the wall containing some of the household crockery. It was here where the old altar table, we saw in the church, did service as a bench.

While resting here, late one day in the autumn we were much amused by the conversation of some farmers and shepherds from Langstrothdale

and Littondale, who were having a carousal around the little table; two lusty Langstroth chaps occupied the old settle in the corner of the fireplace, while

three or four large dogs stretched at full length lay on the floor in front of a big, blazing log fire.

Farmer Johnson had asked them all to drink to the health of the King [*Edward VII*] and Queen and all the Royal family in a neat little toast; after which, Billy got up and moved the "Army, Navy and Reserve Forces in these words - "Gentlemen, t'army an navy hev been drunk for many years, and t'volunteers hev been drunk for nearly half a century, an' may they all be drunk as long as iver Britannia rules the waves." When he sat down again he could not understand the reason why the company laughed so heartily.

Then Farmer Wilson pulling out a handful of money said, "Nah then will yo all hev a drink wi me afoor I go, wot'l thou hev Jack?"

"Hauf a quatern o' whiskey." [*incorrect spelling*] Jack answered.

"An thee Sammy, wots thy usual?"

"Let me hev t'same."

"An thee, Billy what will tha wet thi wissal wi?"

"Well really, farmer, I don't knaw, but ah think I'll hev a mahthful o'whisky [*correct spelling*]."

Billy's mouth is extraordinary and when you see it open its like looking down Douk cave. Noa wonder then that farmer Wilson exclaimed when Billy said he [*would*] have a mouthful, "Nay, tha duzn't, owd man; thah'l hev hawf a quarter like t'rest."

Assuming a "quarter" is quarter of a pint or standard gill, "half-a-quarter" or one-eighth of a pint is a lot of whisky. But it is actually the same as the old Scots whisky measure of 1/4 gill, since in Scotland (and the north of England) a gill is 1/2 a pint, not the standard 1/4 pint, so that 1/4 gill equals 1/8 pint as above. But why did not the George Inn drinkers relate the measure to a gill or even say "half a noggin"? A noggin is a 1/4 pint of spirits and equals the standard English gill. Quarters of whisky were drunk by the British in India.

Looking up Langstrothdale [94]

Leaving the old Inn we tramp the road up Langstrothdale towards Raisgill and Oughtershaw. It is a fine ramble and we simply revel in the wild prospect around us. This romantic valley was an old Forest of the Percies and Cliffords, and in 1241 [*700 years before my stay in Buckden*] William de Percy had then seven lodges for his foresters in this lonely valley of Langstrothdale. At one time it is said that squirrels could spring from tree to tree from here to Netherside, [*Grassington*] without once touching the ground; so dense was the forest in days gone by.

94

95

The Winding Road (Looking down Langstrothdale) [95]

The scenery becomes more austere, but it has no sign of awe-inspiring grandeur. A rough road, deserted of all human traffic, follows the river's course at some elevation above it. On each side is a mossy wall, from which rises the pastureland on our left. (This view was taken looking down the dale.) A young swell of a cyclist recently had a most miraculous escape from death. He was riding like mad down the steep and winding road; when in turning one of the dangerous bends he almost collided with two calves, which seemed to have taken possession of the whole of the narrow roadway. Meeting the farmer at the next turn he jumped off his machine and enquired if "he had lost two calves?"

The old farmer eyeing him quietly over, and taking good stock of his thin shapeless legs, - which very much resembled two sticks of pencil encased in stockings, replied - "No! young man, I don't knaw as I hev lost two calves, but thoo looks as if thoo hed."

Raisgill (Langstrothdale) [96]

Raisgill. This is a hamlet of, perhaps, not more than a couple of cottages, with their bits of garden abutting on the road. These grey walls shielded by gaunt trees add variety to the scene. The hill seen in the background is Yockenthwaite

Fell. (This view I took from the back of the cottages, after crossing over the horse head pass from Halton Gill, looking across the valley). Raisgill is at the junction for the Horse head pass leading over the mountainous ridge to the hamlet of Halton Gill, at the head of Littondale. From this side the bridle track is not so easy to find, and is more difficult to follow, and also more steep than from the other side.

Yockenthwaite (Langstrothdale)

[97]

Leaving Raisgill slumbering among the trees we turn our steps toward Yockenthwaite, which stands pleasantly on the north side of the river. Its mountain summit of 2109 feet rises two miles behind. Here are three houses and no more, a trinity of families in one settlement, with old grey walls, and time worn roofs covered with rich tinted moss, shaded by the spreading branches of fine trees, remnants of a vast forest of oaks, which spread in olden times far over the chase on either side.

Yockenthwaite Bridge [98]

Upwards the country becomes more wild. We are now in the very remoteness of 'Langster'. Langstrath is a very suitable name for the long valley extending

from Buckden to Cam Fell. Note the rocky nature of the river bed; one mass of solid limestone rock, beautifully relieved with green tinted moss. The river here pours down a rocky channel; and in the storms of autumn, when gloom and misty vapours and dark clouds chase across Kirkgill moor, hiding Raisgill Hag and the Horse head pass, the scene is wildly grand. At such times numerous streams, like streaks of silver leap headlong from the mountain in a series of miniature cascades in their course toward the river. Rocks of various formations beset all the river's upper course, imparting a different character to the dale every few leagues - savage, romantic, picturesque and beautiful.

Deepdale old bridge [90]

Presently we come to Deepdale, a most romantic out-of-the world spot, with a very old quaint bridge, near which the river bed is one shelf of solid rock. Soon we observe the Cow Side Farm, on the south side of the river, on a shelving bank, known as hippin' stone hill; a desolate looking place, beneath the upland sheep pastures.

Deepdale old Bridge is a most appropriate setting to the landscape and seems to have grown into its present position; it is an old relic in the dale. On the east side, quite close to the old bridge, there has this year (1907) been a new bridge built, quite close to, in fact, almost touching the old bridge. (Since these notes were written the old Bridge has been destroyed and removed.) *The foundations of the old bridge are visible upstream on the north side.*

Deepdale New Bridge [90]

I am pleased to relate that I was the first passenger across; driving down the dale on Oct. 7th 1907 with the mail carrier, he was privileged by the builders to be the first to drive a vehicle across. We had an interesting little ceremony and I was requested to make a speech, a sort of unofficial opening of the new bridge. Then we

drank success, – good health, – long life &c in a decoction made from malt and hops, which the carrier had brought with him in a stone gallon bottle. Speaking of decoctions, reminds me of an old farmer, who after a days enjoyment at a neighbouring village fair, where he had been taking too liberally of "mountain dew" found himself next morning in the lock-up, having been placed there the night previous, by the village constable.

Eventually he was brought before the magistrate; when the Clerk requested him to "Kiss the book" he said "Nay, lad, nay! for forty years ah'v nivver kiss'd onnybody but my Hatty, an ah'm nooan gooin' ta start nah."

"What's your name ?" thundered the magistrate.

"What?" said the farmer.

"What's your name ?"

"Cain yer honnor."

"What's that you say?"

"Cain yer worship;"

"Cain! – Humpt! and are you that scoundrel who slew his brother Abel?"

"No, sir, I'se sure I isn't; I'm the man as got slewed."

Mail-carriers Signal [101]

This is not at all a pictorial photograph, nevertheless it is a very interesting one to me. Driving down the dale with the mail carrier on the occasion previously mentioned my curiosity was aroused when we came opposite this pile of stones, which is nothing more nor less than a sheep-fold, for my driver pulled up his horse and exclaimed "t' signal's up." He jumped out of the trap, ran round the wall, returning shortly with some letters in his hand, then went back and took down the signal. (This thin black line is the signal, an old rusty sword blade; a thing one would never expect to see in these parts.) - which he laid on the ground.

Resuming our journey, I said, in a sort of an enquiring tone, that that was the most primitive letter posting place I had ever seen. There was no box with lock and key as I have seen in some of the out of way places. He replied, that he collected letters from there twice a week. That is, when the sword blade gave him the signal that a letter had been placed in a nick of the wall. I enquired who put the letters there for there were no houses anywhere to be seen, and he

101

replied, "the people from the farms on the hills above us." Next morning I came up here by myself, to see if the signal was up, but it wasn't, and I had walked about five miles; so not to be outdone I stuck it up, and took this photograph as a record. As I could see no letters in the wall I placed the trusty, I mean rusty sword blade carefully on the ground where I had found it. *For many years there has been a pillar box here and also a telephone box.*

The confluence of the Becks [102]

The confluence of the Becks, with the hamlet of Beckermonds in the background. This is the commencement proper of the river Wharfe, where the two main feeders of this beautiful river unite. The principal of these streams comes down the wildly-beautiful glen of

Oughtershaw, while the other descends from Greenfield Knot, the western limit of the grand old chase of Langstrath.

Memorial Fountain [103]

Turning northwards we ascend the uphill road to Oughtershaw, passing on the way a most welcome, road side resting place and drinking fountain. A tablet of brass attached to the rocks informs us that -

"In remembrance of their mother's first visit to Oughtershaw 12th August 1853. This well was placed here by their son Charles H. L. Wood and Lydia his wife." "Whosoever drinketh of this water shall thirst again" John, ch. IV. v. 13. "If any man thirst let him come unto me and drink." John, ch. VII. v. 37.

The tablet is no longer there.

Oughtershaw Hall (Looking across the moors) [104]

While resting here we obtain a most extensive view of some of Yorkshire's grandest, and wildest scenery, the high moorlands. The track in the distance, stretching across the hill tops leads down into Hawes in Wensleydale over Fleet Moss. *This has long been a metalled road over which coaches now travel.* Amongst the tree tops we just get a peep of Oughtershaw Hall, a handsome and well fit up building. The whole estate, extending to the source of the river on Cam Fell, is the property of the Rev. Trevor Basil Woodd, M.A., L.L.B., vicar of St. Peters, Buckingham Gate, London, eldest son of the late Charles H. L. Woodd, just mentioned. *His will c.1945 states that he was vicar of St. John's, Fitzroy Sq. from 1911 to 1940. During my war-time evacuation to Buckden during 1941, while doing forestry work on the estate, I got to know Rev. Basil Woodd (the same person) who was the last member of the family to live there. It is still (1997) a private house. The bicycle shown is of surprisingly modern (1950s) design.*

School Oughtershaw [105]

The village looks a model of cleanness and comfort, with its pretty school house. On Sundays service is held here; the nearest church is at Hubberholme, six miles distant. *This was a school until Octber 1959; in July 1997 it appeared to be a workshop.*

Swarthgill (the highest House in W. Dale 1300 ft.) [106]

Through the village, we leave the mountain road and make tracks across the fells; some distance above Oughtershaw we come to the lonely farm of Swarthgill, the last inhabited house in the

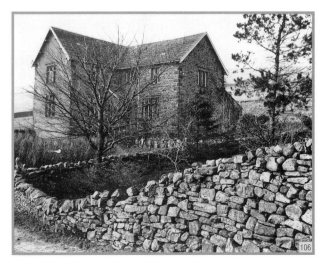

valley and the highest within the watershed of the Wharfe. Its altitude is about 1,300 feet. *There is a print, but no slide, of Nethergill the last house but one in Langstrothdale. This and Swarthgill are farms and on one of these in 1942 I made hay.* Leaving Swarthgill with a parting salute from the cheery hale old farmer, and a warning to - "tak care we dinna get lost," we strike across the trackless moorland of the mighty Cam Fells toward Ribblehead.

Cattle On the Cam Fells [107]

Having conducted you to the head of the Wharfe we will now retrace our steps towards Buckden. *The long horns of the cattle in this slide are interesting since northen cattle have short horns. But these are shaped more like those of Highland cattle than of southern longhorns.*

Tired out (waiting the Mail) [108]

Tired out, after a long day's tramp, we welcome a little rest on the village green at Buckden, and await the arrival of the Mail [*Coach*] to give us a more speedy journey homewards. We are ten miles from the railway station & we feel we have done sufficient walking for the day. Villagers soon gather round, and with them comes the constable to have a little chat with strangers. *There are still two seats in this position.*

Buck Inn. Buckden [109]

As late as the 1950s the motorbus stood in same spot. The sound of horses hoofs, and the rumbling of wheels on the hard limestone road, announces the approach of the mail. It is our signal to be off, - bidding good day to the villagers we take our seat on the front alongside the driver we have met before many times. He is a cheerful chap, always smiling, - (is Tom Smith; he is thoughtful and obliging, and a most trusty and careful driver.) - and we soon engage in conversation relating our days wanderings. *He used to stay at Hartrigg the home of Tom Smith on the edge of the village, which is still a guest house.*

Tom Smith the coachdriver and "Hartrigg" his home

[110, 111]

As twilight approaches the coach speeds on to Starbotton and Kettlewell, collecting the mails, and taking in passengers, then on across the Skirfare Bridge where we take another lingering look up Littondale.

110

111

Evening up Littondale [112]

Daylight is fast fading, and the drive down to Grassington changes its fashion altogether soon as dusk has fallen. The little villages are points of light upon the darkness. The coach lamps throw strange gleams and fluttering shadows on road and limestone walls, and the night comes heavy hearted down the fells.

Here then I must bid adieu to the dale whose beauties I have attempted to describe, and whose attractions I have briefly enumerated.

Its romantic surroundings, its historical associations, and its strange legendry tales and traditions cannot but afford ample food for after reflection, and the rambler who can rightly appreciate the varied attractions possessed by this most favoured valley will carry away impressions that in after life will tend to charm, soothe and sustain the mind, impressions which the heart will cherish among its most precious memories.

the fells.

Here then I must bid adieu
to the dale whose beauties I have
attempted to describe, and whose
attractions I have briefly enumerated.

Its romantic surroundings,
its historical associations, and its
strange legendry tales and traditions
cannot but afford ample food
for after reflection, and the rambler
who can rightly appreciate the varied
attractions possessed by this most favoured
valley will carry away impressions that
in after life will tend to charm, sooth
and sustain the mind, impressions
which the heart will cherish among
its most precious memories.

&

Revised.

Springfield Mount.
Whingate.
Upper Armley,
Leeds. 12.

Thomas Ryder.
October 12th 1907.

91

Thomas Ryder

Revised October 12th 1907

Springfield Mount,

Whingate,

Upper Armley,

Leeds, 12.

⁓

[Only five days after opening of Deepdale bridge, slide 100, p.81]

Some of the Places where I have given my Lecture, and number of times.

Armley. Recreation Club.	1.
" S.t Bartholomews Church. Institute.	2.
" Wesleyian Church School	2.
" " Mission	1.
" Armley & Wortley. P.S. Station Road Mission room.	1.
" " " " West-Leeds High School. Whingate.	3.
" Baptist Church School. Carr Crofts.	1.
Beeston. Church School.	1.
Bradford. Photographic Society.	2.
" P.S. + College of Arts + Crafts.	1.
Batley. Photographic Society.	2.
Brighouse. Camera Club.	2.
Dewsbury. Photographic Soc. Moot-Hall.	2.
Farnley. (old) Church Institute	1.
Halifax. Athletic + Cricket-Club.	2.
" Photographic + Literary Soc.	2.
Huddersfield. Photo + Antiquarian Soc. Technical College.	2.
Leeds. Photographic Soc. Cookridge Street.	1.
" Camera Club. Leeds Institute + Literary Soc.	2.
" Caroline Street. Methodist School.	1.

Leeds. Municipal Officers Guild. Education Large Hall.   1.

"   Leather Manuf^{rs}, & Shoe Makers Guild.   1.

Liversedge. Spen Valley, Literary, Scientific,   2.
           and Photographic Soc. Healds Hall.

New Wortley. Zion Sunday School.   2.

"   "   Whitehall Road, Methodist School.   1.

Otley. Church Institute & Literary Soc.   2.

Rodley and Calverley. P.S.   2.

Wortley. Institute & Choral Soc.   1.

Pudsey. P.S. Mechanics Institute.   2.

Leeds. Oxford Place Chapel — School room.   1.

Armley. Parochial Hall. Ridge Road.   1.
       (Armley District Nursing Fund.)

Armley. Temperance Hall. Wesley Road.   1.
        A.W.D.Soc.

Armley. Methodist Guild.   1.

Then and Now

A selection of photographs
taken by Barrie Pepper in 2002.

Thomas Ryder's photographs, taken
from the text, are shown first.

Contents

Ancient Archway (Bolton Abbey)

Barden Tower

Percival Hall

Monks Hall (Appletreewick)

Appletreewick (looking down the village)

Red Lion Hotel (Burnsall)

Burnsall Grammar School

Burnsall Bridge

Threshfield Grammar School

The Market Place (Grassington)

47

Netherside Hall

Tennant Arms (Kilnsey)

56

Kilnsey Crag (then)

Kilnsey Crag (now)

Conistone Church

The Queen's Arms (Litton)

Blue Bell (Kettlewell)

Kettlewell Church

Fox and Hounds (Starbotton)

Hubberholme Church

The George Inn (Kirkgill)

105

Oughtershaw School

Buck Inn (Buckden)